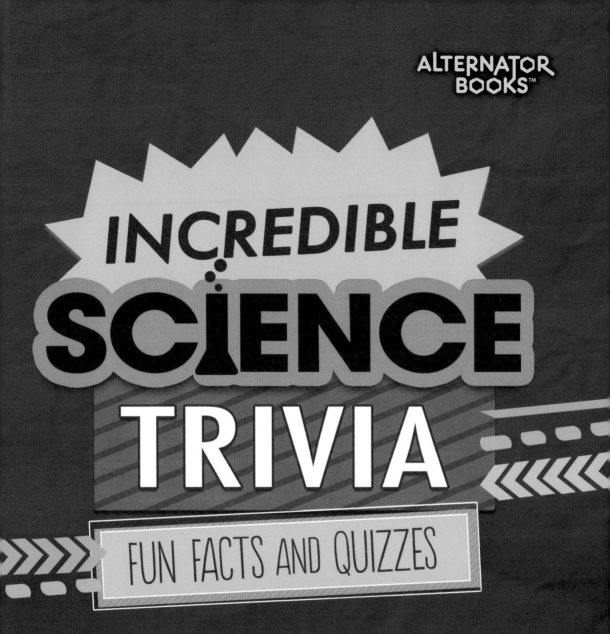

INCREDIBLE SCIENCE TRIVIA

FUN FACTS AND QUIZZES

Heather E. Schwartz

Lerner Publications ◆ Minneapolis

ALTERNATOR
BOOKS™

Lerner Publications Company
A division of Lerner Publishing Group, Inc.
241 First Avenue North
Minneapolis, MN 55401 USA

For reading levels and more information, look up this title at www.lernerbooks.com.

Main body text set in Aptifer Slab LT Pro Regular.
Typeface provided by Linotype AG.

Library of Congress Cataloging-in-Publication Data

Names: Schwartz, Heather E., author.
Title: Incredible science trivia : fun facts and quizzes / by Heather E. Schwartz.
Description: Minneapolis : Lerner Publications, [2018] | Series: Trivia time! | Audience: Age 8–12. | Audience: Grade 4 to 6. | Includes bibliographical references.
Identifiers: LCCN 2017018455 (print) | LCCN 2017026368 (ebook) | ISBN 9781512483376 (eb pdf) | ISBN 9781512483345 (lb : alk. paper)
Subjects: LCSH: Science—Miscellanea—Juvenile literature.
Classification: LCC Q173 (print) | LCC Q173 .S3935 2018 (ebook) | DDC 500—dc23

LC record available at https://lccn.loc.gov/2017018455

Manufactured in the United States of America
1-43341-33161-9/7/2017

CONTENTS

AROUND YOUR HOME

Most modern toilets use 1.6 gallons (6 L) of water each time you flush. This sounds like a lot, but some old toilets used as much as 3.5 gallons (13 L) per flush!

Q: Microwave ovens heat up food fast. But how?

A: They cause water, fat, and sugar molecules to vibrate about 2.5 trillion times per second. That motion creates heat to cook food.

Besides washing dishes, dish soap can safely be used for

A. Killing weeds
B. Killing ants
C. Washing hair
D. All of the above

The answer is D. For weed killing, the combination is 1 teaspoon of dish soap, 1 cup of salt, and 1 gallon (3.8 L) of white vinegar. For ant killing, the mixture is equal amounts of water and white vinegar and a splash of dish soap. And to wash your hair, mix a bit of dish soap with your shampoo—it fights grease in your hair just as it does on dishes.

Swimming in the ocean isn't as dangerous as sticking a fork or knife in the toaster. Malfunctioning toasters kill about 700 people each year. Sharks kill only about six.

House dust is a combination of insect waste, human skin, dirt, sand, and—in homes with pets—pet hair or skin. Yuck!

The average kitchen counter has about 1,700 bacteria per square inch (6.5 sq. cm). To be sanitary—or clean enough to eat off—it should have no more than

A. 25
B. 50
C. 100
D. 1,000

The answer is D. That may be more than you thought! But thinking about any bacteria on your counter can be pretty gross. To bring the bacteria count down, simply spray the counter with disinfectant or vinegar.

Unless it's brand new, your kitchen sponge is likely loaded with more than 200,000 bacteria per square inch. It's actually much dirtier than the average toilet seat.

IN YOUR BODY

Laugh your troubles away. Scientists say laughing is actually good for your heart. It increases blood flow, decreases stress hormones, and boosts your immune system so you can fight off illness.

Nose shape is determined by more than genes. Your nose may also develop to work with the climate you live in. People in warmer climates often have wider nostrils than people in colder climates. One reason might be that narrower nostrils help to warm up air as it enters the body.

Q: When humans are born, they have about 300 bones in their body. By the time they grow up, they have only 206. How can that be?

A: Some bones fuse together as a baby grows. These include bones in the skull and the spine.

Q: Is there a scientific reason why some people are couch potatoes?

A: Yes! A specific gene might be to blame—but that's no excuse for lazy behavior. Your body still needs exercise, even if your brain doesn't send the signals that will motivate you to get moving.

You know the colors of the rainbow. But how many total colors do you think the human eye can see?

A. 7
B. 100
C. 1,000
D. 1 million

It's D—some people can even see 100 million colors! These people are called tetrachromats.

Darker skin contains more melanin, a pigment that colors the skin, eyes, and hair. Melanin offers protection from the sun's ultraviolet rays. But don't skip the sunscreen. You can still get a burn even if you have a dark complexion or a tan.

Bad haircut? Don't fret. Hair grows about

A. Half an inch (1.3 cm) each month
B. A quarter inch (0.6 cm) each month
C. Half an inch every three months
D. A quarter inch every three months

The answer is A. That's 6 inches (15 cm) per year!

NATURE NEWS

There are more than 80,000 edible plants on Earth. They include weeds, flowers, and seeds—but don't pick and eat a plant unless you're sure. Plants can be poisonous and even deadly.

Earth looks perfectly round from space, but it isn't. It's an oblate spheroid. So it is a little like a squished ball—it's wider in the middle.

Ever seen a triple or quadruple rainbow? They do exist, but they're extremely rare. Only four or five have been documented since 1700.

Bamboo grows faster than any other plant. How many inches do you think it can grow in a day?

A. 5 inches (13 cm)
B. 10 inches (25 cm)
C. 25 inches (64 cm)
D. 35 inches (89 cm)

Did you say D? You're right! That's almost 3 feet (0.9 m), or about the height from the bottom of a door to the doorknob.

Q: How long can a tree live?

A: Trees can live thousands of years. One bristlecone pine in California's White Mountains is more than 5,000 years old. And there are quaking aspen trees in Utah that scientists estimate are more than 80,000 years old.

Green grass isn't just pretty. It produces oxygen too. How much? Each 650 square foot (200 sq. m) area of grass releases enough oxygen to sustain one human adult.

How many seeds do you think an average strawberry has?

A. 100
B. 150
C. 200
D. 300

The answer is B. Whew! Good thing you don't have to count them yourself!

ALL ABOUT ANIMALS

Why does a bull charge at a matador's flapping red cape?

A. Bulls hate bright colors.
B. Bulls hate the color red.
C. The movement of the cape bothers the bull.
D. Bulls hate capes.

You might be surprised to find out it's C. The color of the cape doesn't matter—bulls are color-blind.

Squid and octopuses have three hearts. One pumps blood through the body. The other two pump blood to the gills so the blood can pick up oxygen.

The world's oldest cat, according to the *Guinness World Records*, lived to be

A. 17 years old
B. 24 years old
C. 38 years old
D. 96 years old

C, Crème Puff the cat was born in 1967 and died in 2005.

Q: Why do bats sleep upside down?

A: It's relaxing for them. They don't have to contract any muscles to hang, so it actually uses less energy than sitting right side up. It's also easy for them to launch from upside down right into flight.

Q: Are sloths really the laziest animal?

A: Sloths sleep a lot—about nine to 10 hours a day—but they don't sleep more than any other animal. Koalas spend about 14 hours each day asleep, and some bats sleep 20 hours a day.

Mind Blown

Q: Can dogs learn to read?

A: Many dogs can be taught to follow written commands such as *jump* and *speak*. They learn to recognize the shapes of the words, which is very much like reading.

WHAT A DISASTER

Q: What's the tallest wave ever measured?

A: The tallest documented tsunami came from Alaska's Lituya Bay. When it crashed onto shore, it destroyed trees 1,700 feet (518 m) above sea level.

Fish falling from the sky? Blame a tornado. They sometimes lift animals such as fish, frogs, and alligators out of the water and drop them on land.

Q: How many earthquakes are there each year?

A: Some scientists think there are probably millions— but most are too small to feel or even detect with scientific instruments.

Hawaii's Kilauea volcano has been erupting continuously since 1983. The lava it spews can reach 1,650°F (899°C). That's hotter than

A. The temperature on Mercury
B. The temperature on Venus
C. The highest temperature ever recorded in Death Valley National Park
D. All of the above

The answer is D. Mercury can reach 801°F (427°C) during the day. Venus has an average temperature of 864°F (462°C). The highest temperature ever recorded in Death Valley was 134°F (56°C), in 1913.

Forest fires burn through 4 to 5 million acres (1.6 to 2 million ha) of land in the United States each year. A wildfire can spread fast, burning through everything in its path at a speed of 14 miles (23 km) an hour.

A powerful storm with strong winds that starts over the ocean is called

A. A hurricane
B. A cyclone
C. A typhoon
D. All of the above

It's D. These storms are called by different names in different places, depending on where they start. Hurricanes come from the Atlantic and Northeast Pacific. Cyclones start in the South Pacific and Indian Ocean. Typhoons originate in the Northwest Pacific.

HOW WOULD LIFE BE DIFFERENT IN SPACE?

You might get taller.

The spine expands in low gravity. Astronauts grow up to 3 percent taller while they're in space.

You'd have to swallow your toothpaste.

There are no sinks, and anyway, if you tried to spit after brushing your teeth in space, the foamy toothpaste would just float everywhere.

If you cried, your tears wouldn't fall.

Weaker gravity would cause them to pool in a ball of water on your face.

You'd have to be extra active.

Floating around in space causes loss of muscle strength. Astronauts in space exercise for 2.5 hours six days a week.

You wouldn't enjoy your food as much.

The fluids in your body would rise up and clog your sinuses as if you had a cold or allergies. That makes it more difficult to smell and taste food.

You'd never burp.

Or rather, you'd never burp without throwing up too. Gas can't rise above the contents of your stomach in space. One burp brings up everything in there with it.

WATER WORLD

You've heard of acid rain, right? Well, rain isn't the only precipitation that can be acidic. Snow, fog, and hail can be acidic too.

The Mpemba effect is the name for which phenomenon?

A. Ice doesn't melt.
B. Cold water doesn't freeze.
C. Hot water doesn't freeze.
D. Hot water freezes faster than cold water.

The answer is D. It was named after a Tanzanian boy who was making ice cream and found boiling milk froze faster than cooled milk.

Thousands of algae, protozoans, bacteria, and viruses live in one drop of untreated water.

Q: How long can a person survive without water?

A: That depends on the environment. A strong, healthy person could live for more than a week in some cases. But if it's very hot, a person might die within hours.

Q: How much salt is in Earth's oceans?

A: If we could take it out of the sea and put it on land, it would be more than 500 feet (152 m) wide and as tall as a 40-story building.

Why does ocean water look blue?

A. It reflects the sky.
B. The ocean floor is blue.
C. Ocean water absorbs other colors more strongly than blue.
D. The ocean contains many blue rocks.

If you guessed C, you're right! Water absorbs red, orange, and yellow light, so the blue shows more.

About 8 million tons (7 million t) of plastic are dumped in the ocean each year.

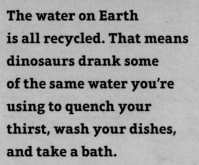

Mind Blown

The water on Earth is all recycled. That means dinosaurs drank some of the same water you're using to quench your thirst, wash your dishes, and take a bath.

17

INSECT SCIENCE

There are 10 quintillion living insects on Earth at all times. That's more than a billion, trillion, or quadrillion.

Praying mantises are carnivores that usually eat other insects but can also eat small birds, amphibians, and reptiles.

Termites are attracted to the smell of ink from a ballpoint pen. It reminds them of the trails they usually leave to help them find food. If you draw a maze on a paper and set down some termites, they'll walk along the pen line, expecting to find food at the end.

Q: What makes a Mexican jumping bean jump?

A: The bean, which is really a seedpod, contains a moth larva. When the larva moves, so does the bean. The larva will eventually spin a cocoon inside the pod and leave as an adult moth.

Q: Are ants the strongest insects in the world?

A: Ants can lift 50 times their own body weight. But the *Onthophagus taurus*, a species of horned dung beetle, is even stronger. It can pull 1,141 times its own weight. That's like a 50-pound (23 kg) kid pulling two large school buses.

Adult mayflies don't live long at all. They may live for only a few minutes or for as long as two days.

How many silkworms does it take to make 1 pound (0.5 kg) of silk?

A. 20
B. 200
C. 2,500
D. 20,000

C is the correct answer. Many silkworms work on farms in China and India. The silk is used to make clothing, tires, electronics, and military supplies.

CHEW ON THIS!

The weight, size, shape, and color of the utensils you use makes a difference in how you experience your food. For example, yogurt can seem creamier eaten with a glass utensil compared to a plastic spoon.

Good food smells such as ham or vanilla can trick your brain into believing you're eating salt or sugar—even when you're not.

The right texture could convince you low-salt potato chips taste just like the regular kind. There's a whole science devoted to food texture, called food rheology.

The brain links food color with food flavor. In one experiment, people reported an orange-colored drink tasted like orange, even though it was actually cherry flavored.

Food tastes better when eaten from a white plate. This may be because food looks more brightly colored against the white background.

A large container can convince you to eat more. In one study, people were served popcorn in either a medium or large container. All ate more from the large container, even when the popcorn was stale.

IN SCHOOL

A playground swing is a kind of

A. Pendulum
B. Lever
C. Pulley
D. Gear

A pendulum is a weight hung from a fixed point. It swings back and forth due to the force of gravity, so the answer is A.

Certain parts of the brain get bigger when you learn to play a musical instrument. And these areas do more than control musical abilities. They also make you better at math!

Q: Do pencils make their mark with lead?

A: No, they're filled with a combination of clay and graphite, a crystallized form of carbon. The average pencil contains enough of this mixture to write a line 35 miles (56 km) long.

Q: Does it take a lot of trees to make paper?

A: More than you'd think. About 4 tons (3.6 t) of wood go into the creation of 1 ton (0.9 t) of paper.

The globe was invented by

A. Nicolaus Copernicus
B. Martin Behaim
C. Crates of Mallus
D. Christopher Columbus

It's C, the Greek Crates of Mallus. He created the first 3-D model of Earth more than 2,000 years ago. But the oldest surviving globe was made by Martin Behaim in 1492.

Bored in class? That's not necessarily a bad thing. Studies show boredom can inspire creative ideas, push you to try new things, and even make you a nicer person.

Need one more reason to call physical education class your favorite part of the school day? Exercise is good for the body and the mind. It can help you grow new brain cells.

HEALTHFUL LIVING

Wearing shorts when it's cold outside won't give you a cold. But you could get hypothermia or frostbite. Ready to rethink that fashion statement?

Q: Is there any way to make shots hurt less?

A: Studies have shown you can do many things to reduce the ouch factor. Beforehand, relax with deep breaths and rub the spot the doctor is aiming for. During the injection, distract yourself by singing or talking. Afterward, don't touch or rub the spot. Leave it alone to heal.

Keeping your teeth healthy can be costly and time consuming. Americans buy 14 million gallons (53 million L) of toothpaste each year. On average, Americans spend 38.5 days during their lifetime brushing their teeth.

Which statement about bacteria is true?

A. Most bacteria is more helpful than harmful.
B. Some bacteria can eat sweat.
C. Only 1 percent of bacteria leads to disease in humans.
D. All of the above are true.

The answer is D.

Q: Why do we have eyebrows?

A: They catch rain and sweat before they can get into your eyes. They show emotion. And they also help with facial recognition. Without them, humans would not be able to recognize one another easily.

When it comes to water, too much can be just as bad for you as too little. It can cause

A. Hypothermia
B. Hyponatremia
C. Hyperbole
D. Hyperactivity

It's B—hyponatremia can cause vomiting, headache, loss of energy, and even death.

CRAZY CURES

Modern treatments sure beat those of the past! Ancient doctors attempted to cure patients by these methods:

Boring holes in the skull (called trepanation)

Cutting the skin or applying leeches to let out the "bad blood" (called bloodletting)

Offering medicines made of poisonous or gross ingredients, such as mercury, human blood, and crushed mummies

Applying dead mice, animal poop, or moldy bread to the skin

Suggesting they sleep next to—and kiss—a human skull

These so-called cures often killed people. But some of them actually worked! For example, animal poop can act as an antibiotic. Who knew!?

TRUE OR FALSE

Now that you're an expert in science trivia, test yourself further with these true or false questions. You can find the answers at the bottom of page 29.

1. There are millions of insect species still waiting to be discovered.

2. The longest word in the English language is the chemical name of the largest known protein.

3. Footprints left by astronauts on the moon in 1969 will never wear away.

4. Cats have more taste buds than humans.

5. In 2011 a 10-year-old became the youngest person to discover a supernova.

6. All humans are 99.9 percent genetically identical.

7. Moose have to sleep standing up.

8. In 2013 part of Florida's Walt Disney World fell into a sinkhole.

9. The first living being to orbit Earth was a dog.

10. The human hand has more bones than the human foot.

1) True. 2) True. It has 189,819 letters. 3) False. Scientists predict they will take 10 to 100 million years to wear away. 4) False. Cats have 473. Humans have 9,000. 5) True. 6) True. 7) False. They can sleep lightly standing up, but they have to lie down for a deeper sleep. 8) False. A resort 10 minutes from Walt Disney World fell into the sinkhole. 9) True. Laika, in 1957. 10) True. The hand has 27 bones. The foot has 26.

WHO KNEW!?

By definition, trivia is just a bunch of useless information. But here's proof trivia is big business, a popular pastime, and even a great workout for your brain!

- The board game Trivial Pursuit was invented in 1979. In 1984, 24 million copies of the game were sold in the United States.

- Answering trivia questions correctly can stimulate your body to produce dopamine, a feel-good chemical.

- Students at the University of Wisconsin–Stevens Point host the world's largest trivia contest each year. It starts with a parade and ends 54 hours later.

- Playing trivia games is like exercising your brain. It improves your memory and helps keep your brain young and healthy.

- The trivia game show *Jeopardy!* has been on TV since 1964.

FURTHER INFORMATION

Ecology Kids
http://www.ecology.com/ecology-kids

Hanna, Jack. *Jack Hanna's Wild but True: Amazing Animal Facts You Won't Believe!* New York: Media Lab Books, 2016.

NASA Kids' Club
https://www.nasa.gov/kidsclub/index.html

National Geographic. *Weird but True: Human Body.* Washington, DC: National Geographic, 2017.

Pew Research Center: Science Knowledge Quiz
http://www.pewresearch.org/quiz/science-knowledge

Schwartz, Heather E. *Incredible Tech Trivia: Fun Facts and Quizzes.* Minneapolis: Lerner Publications, 2018.

Time. *Time for Kids Big Book of Why.* New York: Liberty Street, 2016.

PHOTO ACKNOWLEDGMENTS

The images in this book are used with the permission of: iStock.com/desertsolitaire, p. 4; iStock.com/Violetastock, p. 5 (top); iStock.com/somchaisom, p. 5 (bottom); iStock.com/Ale-ks, pp. 6–7 (background); iStock.com/RusN, p. 6; iStock.com/keithpix, p. 7 (top); iStock.com/Jason_V, p. 7 (bottom); iStock.com/drferry, pp. 8–9 (background); iStock.com/celafon, p. 8; iStock.com/AlexStar, p. 9; iStock.com/TheSP4N1SH, pp. 10–11 (background); iStock.com/caughtinthe, p. 11 (top); iStock.com/Julesru, p. 11 (bottom); iStock.com/AZ68, pp. 12–13 (background); iryna1/Shutterstock.com, p. 12; NASA/JSC, pp. 14, 15; iStock.com/Hydromet, pp. 16–17 (background); Rattiya Thongdumhyu/Shutterstock.com, p. 16; metha1819/Shutterstock.com, p. 17; iStock.com/Cabezonication, pp. 18–19 (background); iStock.com/dreamnikon, p. 18; iStock.com/esolla, p. 19; SabOlga/Shutterstock.com, p. 20 (top); iStock.com/yalcinsonat1, p. 20 (bottom); iStock.com/ValentynVolkov, p. 21 (top); iStock.com/NatashaPhoto, p. 21 (bottom); iStock.com/matt_benoit, pp. 22–23 (center); iStock.com/LeventKonuk, p. 22; iStock.com/Steve Debenport, p. 23; iStock.com/Henrik5000, pp. 24–25 (background); iStock.com/serezniy, p. 24 (top); iStock.com/marieclaudelemay, p. 24 (bottom); iStock.com/Mik122, p. 25 (top); iStock.com/eurobanks, p. 25 (bottom left); iStock.com/yamahavalerossi, p. 25 (bottom right); iStock.com/Eugene03, p. 26; iStock.com/eag1e, p. 27 (top); iStock.com/ozandogan, p. 27 (bottom). Design elements: R-studio/Shutterstock.com; balabolka/Shutterstock.com.

Front cover: robert_s/Shutterstock.com (globe); Sebastian Kaulitzki/Shutterstock.com (brain); Andrey Pavlov/Shutterstock.com (ant); metha1819/Shutterstock.com (dinosaur); GAZIYEV MEHMAN/Shutterstock.com (atom icon); anthonycz/Shutterstock.com (test tube).